# HOW
# NOT TO GIVE UP

## A MOTIVATIONAL & INSPIRATIONAL GUIDE TO GOAL SETTING & ACHIEVING YOUR DREAMS

FROM THE
*Inspirational*
BOOKS SERIES
— R.L. ADAMS —

### R.L. Adams

# From The

# *Inspirational Book Series*

by

R.L. Adams

- *Breakthrough – Live an Inspired Life, Overcome your Obstacles and Accomplish your Dreams*

- *How to be Happy – An Inspirational Guide to Discovering What Happiness is and How to have More of it in your Life*

- *Have a Little Hope – An Inspirational Guide to Discovering What Hope is and How to have More of it in your Life*

- *How Not to Give Up – A Motivational & Inspirational Guide to Goal Setting & Achieving your Dreams*

- *The Silk Merchant – Ancient Words of Wisdom to Help you Live a Better Life Today*

- *Move Mountains – How to Achieve Anything in your Life with the Power of Positive Thinking*

*This Page Intentionally Left Blank*

# All Rights Reserved

# Legal Notices

*This Page Intentionally Left Blank*

# CONTENTS

# INTRODUCTION

*"In life you need either inspiration or desperation"* — Anthony Robbins

"I give up."

I've given up in my life. I've uttered those three simple words more times than I would like to admit. I never wanted to give up but I did it anyways. I gave up on a lot of things. I gave up on marriage. I gave up on business. I gave up on friends. But worst of all, I gave up on family. I just gave up.

The feeling of giving up has always been somewhat mixed for me, especially when I had given up on goals that were once so important. Looking back, those are the ones that make me want to turn back the hands of time and not give up. Those are the ones that really meant something to me.

It's easy to give up, especially when the going gets

tough. But isn't that what usually happens when the odds are seemingly stacked against you? People just give up, don't they? But, what sets apart that person who perseveres through the tough times, pushes through to achieve their goals, and doesn't give up, from the person who easily falters, and gives up at the slightest sign of resistance?

I know in my life things didn't always come that easy, but looking back at it now, I know I could have worked harder, done more, said more, and at times, learned more. I could have picked myself back up. But instead, my will was weak. I gave up. I stood up, threw in the proverbial towel, and I was done. I wasn't going to do it anymore; I wasn't going to pursue that dream. I couldn't suffer through the failures any longer. It was over. I was finished. Finite. I uttered words like "Adios," "Never again," "That's it," "I quit," "Enough," "I'm done," and of course, "I give up."

Sometimes I gave up in silent resignation, and at other times it was far more pronounced. But none of the times did it ever really feel that good to give up. I never felt whole, complete, or satisfied. Instead, I felt like I had failed. I felt like I had let myself, and everyone else around me down who had believed in me. It wasn't a good feeling. It never was.

Of course giving up doesn't feel good, at least, giving up on something worthwhile, that is. I wouldn't categorize giving up on something that's detrimental to you a bad thing, like smoking cigarettes, or eating too much sugar. But then again, sometimes we're just suckers for punishment, like when we refuse to give up on relationships that are clearly toxic, but keep drawing us back in.

We tend to gravitate back to things that are

comfortable to us because it's what we know – those are the types of things we sometimes need to give up on. I'm not talking about those types of things. What I'm talking about is the fact that, giving up doesn't feel good when it's a hope or dream that you've tirelessly pursued for a long time – something you poured your heart and soul into at one point in your life, and that meant something, something sacred.

After a violent stretch of giving up in my life, one day something happened to me. I'm not sure if you would call it hitting an emotional rock bottom, or coming to some internal epiphany, but whatever it was, it was strong. It was jarring in fact. This "awakening" that happened, allowed me to realize, with pinpoint accuracy, just what I had been doing wrong, and just what it was going to take to make things right.

Today, I couldn't even imagine myself uttering those three words because, something shifted inside of me. It was something profound and truly life altering that happened. When it happened, I felt it. I knew that it had occurred. It was as though my entire psyche had altered. My whole way of thinking changed in what felt like an instant. But it wasn't an instant, it was a series of events that culminated in that very moment, and it's at that very moment that everything changed. I started to not give up.

This is a story about not giving up, even when times are tough. It's a story about our personal journeys to reach for the stars, even when we feel like we can't lift our hands any higher. This is the story of digging down deep inside, and finding the strength buried hidden away even when all hope seems to be lost. This is the story about finding that final strand of inspiration to persevere and achieve.

This is the story of how not to give up.

# 1

## THE MEANING OF GOALS

*"What you get by achieving your goals is not as important as what you become by achieving your goals." – Henry David Thoreau*

"I give up!" I yelled adamantly. I wasn't going to play the piano ever again. I was committed. That was it, not once more I told myself. I glared at the big black monstrosity with a fury that burned hotter than a massive underground coal fire, as I slammed the piano key cover down, shuttering my father's dreams along with it.

"You can't give up!" My father yelled back at me, turning his head to see his eldest son clenching his fists in a fit of rage as I left the room.

"Sure I can. I can do whatever I want!" Storming off, I screamed the words over and over again until I could no longer be heard, stomping up the stairs loudly, as though I were trying to place holes in its wooden steps. I slammed the door loudly behind me. I was 12.

I remember that day like it was yesterday. My father had these big hopes and dreams for me of becoming a concert pianist. He was dead set on it in fact. It had already occurred in his mind because he had envisioned it so hard. He pushed those goals onto me. They weren't my goals, they were his, and no matter what he did or how hard he tried he couldn't coerce me to believe that those goals were my own.

There was no strong meaning or burning desire in my heart to play the piano. I didn't feel any prouder, stronger, or smarter when I sat in front of those keys. In fact, I felt stupid, lazy, and slow, like I couldn't get the song right no matter how hard I tried. Although I tried for him at times to put my heart into it, the passion just wasn't there.

To my father, playing the piano was everything, and in his mind the meaning attributed to being a concert pianist was next to Godliness. But it wasn't for me. It wasn't my goal, my hope, my dream or my desire. So I gave up.

I didn't attribute a strong enough meaning or reason as to why I had to play the piano, so I stopped. I gave up. I didn't believe strongly in it enough. It didn't burn as a passion for me in my heart. I wasn't committed to it like my father was. I didn't have that deep-rooted meaning latched on to it like he did; it just wasn't there for me. It wasn't there so I gave up, just as I had done so on many other things in my life.

I wanted to set my own goals, and determine my own life's path. I wanted to make an impact on the world, and make a difference. I wanted to be someone important. I wanted to be a doctor, or a lawyer, or a rich businessman because to me that meant something. Being a piano player didn't.

After some time had passed and I began to recollect on this I realized that in life, if you can't attach a deep-rooted meaning to your own goals, you'd always give up, just like I did with playing the piano. In your life, you may have given up on some simple things as well, such as playing the piano, or learning a new language. Or maybe, you gave up on something major, things such as a marriage or a career.

Whatever it was that you gave up on, when you gave up it meant that you let go of something that didn't have meaning to you anymore. You may have attributed meaning to it at some point in the past, and there may still be some hidden meaning there somewhere, buried deep inside of you, but it had all but vanished when you quit. Because, when something truly means something to you, and you're able to attribute enough value and reasoning as to why you have to have it or achieve it, then you'll find a way, and you'll find yourself not giving up; you'll find yourself persevering.

So how do you go about giving your goals a strong enough meaning so as to not give up on them? How is that you can take something that once didn't mean something to you, and attribute, and attach a powerful meaning that will help you see your way through it? Maybe the thing that you're going after has value and meaning to you, but it's just buried behind and beneath other things that have more value and meaning to you. Or so you think.

Had I not been just a boy, and piano was a career to me, there could have been a stronger meaning for me to continue playing the piano. If I had attributed my financial survival, and the survival of my family to playing the piano, the value of playing the piano professionally would have increased tremendously in my mind, and I would have never quit. But, back then, it didn't mean that much to me because I was just a kid. How could something mean a lot to a 12 year old boy who's only concerns are doing homework, going to school, eating, sleeping, and spending time with his friends?

However, as an adult, you can find deep meanings for your goals and attribute important aspects of your future success, happiness, and fulfillment to the attainment of a goal if you just allow yourself to reflect further on its real meaning. It simply involves spending some time with yourself to brainstorm just what something means to you. It's as simple as that. However, oftentimes, more so than not, we don't do that do we? We don't take the necessary time to analyze and realize certain aspects of our lives and the things that matter to it. We let things go.

Sometimes we let our finances go, and other times we let our love lives go, and still other times we let our health go. The list can go on and on. But, should you spend the proper time with yourself, by yourself, analyzing yourself, and what motivates you, you will be able to attribute the meaning necessary to see just about anything through in life that matters. It's not as simple as that, but it certainly starts with that.

Meaning is the foundation for success; it's the foundation for not giving up. Anytime you try to half-heartedly approach a goal, you'll fail. Come on, you know exactly what I mean don't you? Think of the times when something just didn't matter to you that much. You knew that you *should* do it but you didn't think that you *must* do it. It has to become a *must* for you, otherwise you'll end up giving up because it doesn't matter to you all that much. If it mattered it would be a *must*.

You may be sitting there thinking, "Sure, I've set some

goals in the past that I really wanted to achieve but I couldn't do it." Even though you thought it was a must for you, you still failed, so what gives? Well, it wasn't a must for you, if it was, you would have succeeded. When something becomes a must, all the obstacles standing in your way fall, like the pillars of a building being toppled over.

When you see an obstacle, or a resistance to your goal, it instantly becomes much harder for you mentally to see yourself achieving it. It doesn't actually become harder; you just think it is, so that's what you manifest in your mind. It becomes significantly more difficult to overcome something that in your mind's eye is built up to be so much more difficult than it is. That's because the mind is an incredibly powerful thing, and no matter what we attribute to it, that will come to pass.

You have to give something meaning in order to overcome any mental barriers in place. There has to be a strong enough will to overcome the potential failures and setbacks you may experience while striving for your goals. Could you imagine if Thomas Edison had quit after 9,000 times of trying to invent the light bulb?

What if Martin Luther King Jr. quit his fight for civil rights in America, how do you think things would look now? What if Abraham Lincoln didn't fight for the slaves? What if Gandhi didn't silently protest for an independent India? What if the Nazis had taken over Europe and won the Second World War? What if the Wright brothers never stuck it out and invented flight? What if we stopped trying to put a man on the moon? What if all these people gave up?

You see, without a strong enough meaning to your goals you won't be able to break through these barriers. You won't be able to overcome obstacles, trample over doubts, and blaze through failures. You'll give up at the slightest sign of resistance.

# FINDING MEANING

Each and every one of us sets goals in life. Some of us do it silently in our minds, while others take to pen and paper, or some digital format. There are those of us out there that harbor grandiose goals involving fortune and fame, and others still that have much more understated goals such as taking moonlit-strolls along the beach with a loved one.

In the past, I was always a chronic goal setter. I would set goals then do what it took to meet those goals. I was able to attribute strong enough meanings to the goals and come up with core reasons why I *had to do it*. I made them musts. I was your typical overachiever for a while. I pushed and prodded my way along achieving everything that I set my heart on.

But then at some point, somewhere along the way I lost my way; I got stuck. I stopped attributing strong meanings to my goals and eventually I stopped setting them altogether, and started living my life as though nothing really mattered. It was a dark spiral downward that didn't seem to have a bottom at the time (or so I thought) but eventually I found it, and I landed flat on my face.

If you're anything like me, then you've set some goals in the past, but you haven't been able to achieve the important ones; you haven't been able to realize those big aspirations and hopes you had for your life. Something has been holding you back. Maybe you just got frustrated along the way like I did. Maybe your priorities changed. Or, maybe you threw up your hands in the air one day in silent resignation. I know I have.

Whatever it was that stopped you from achieving your goals, it just happened, and it's happened to all of us. But those goals are probably still sitting somewhere on a notepad, on your laptop, or maybe even on a crumpled up piece of paper in a drawer somewhere in your house.

What happened to those once so sought after goals? Did they wash away for you in the tide of life? It's okay, it's happened to us all. For me, I just let it go. Those goals sailed off on a ship in a turbulent sea, never to be seen again. The stress and the pressure of life got to me, and I cracked. That was it, and after that day I became an expert on giving up. In fact, I was dead set on never making another goal again for the rest of my life. I'm glad that changed.

To set a goal, and really achieve it in life, those goals need to have a strong enough meaning to us. Those goals sitting on that crumpled up piece of paper in your drawer weren't meaningful enough to achieve, because you didn't attribute a strong enough meaning to them as to why you had to achieve them in the first place. Without this, no goal can be fully attainable, because our internal mechanism does nothing to push us to strive for something we don't wholeheartedly believe in.

Before understanding why you want to achieve something so badly, you have to appreciate the meaning of goals in and of themselves. What does it mean to set a goal for you? Is it something arbitrary that you do in your mind, or do you actually pull out that pen and paper, or launch your notepad on your laptop?

The literal meaning of a goal is an observable and measurable end result with objectives that need to be achieved within a specific time frame. However, the real meaning of a goal is much more profound than this. A goal symbolizes your commitment to something important in your life; something you really believe in.

Most people only engage in goal setting on one day of the year. Yes, you guessed it, New Year's Eve. They have this so-called "New Year's Syndrome" that happens once, and then is almost wholly forgotten about in the blur of the following days, weeks, and months. I'm sure you've had experience with this. I know I have.

I've set goals on New Year's Eve that I thought I was committed to, but I really wasn't. In fact, the times I did fail my New Year's goals were the times I didn't take it seriously. Those were the times that I didn't pull out a pen and paper and write them down, and didn't make the connection of what meaning I attributed to achieving those goals.

But you're not alone in this goal setting dilemma that happens once a year. Here are some statistics about New Year's Syndrome goals:

- 25% give up after just one week of setting the goal.

- 80% give up after 20 days of setting the goal.

- Only 8% stick it out and actually achieve the goal.

Those are some pretty staggering numbers. So what sets the 8% apart that actually make their goal a reality? How do those 8% dig in their heels and push through even when they are faced with temptations to quit? How is that when that chocolate cake is just sitting there and no one else is around that they don't succumb to the temptation? How do they actually push through and not give up?

The people who achieve their New Year's goals are no different than the people who set goals on a daily, weekly, and monthly basis who achieve them; not just once a year. No matter when you set your goal or what that goal is, that goal has to mean something to you; the goal has to be important. If you're setting goals just because it's socially acceptable to set a specific type of goal, you will fail. That goal has to be vital to you.

You might think to yourself, well, you've set goals in the past that were important to you but you still gave up. But, did you really think about it? Did you take the proper steps involved with successful goal setting? Have you ever taken a goal setting workshop and learned how to set goals the right way?

If you feel lost and overwhelmed at times, that's okay, we all do. In the end, if you're looking to not give up on something, then it has to mean something to you. Beyond just the literal meaning of what a goal is, it has to have a deeper, more impactful meaning, inside your heart and soul; you have to believe in it.

Without belief in a goal and your ability to accomplish it, the likelihood of failure will rise. In fact, you might think that a goal is more meaningful to you than it actually is, but if you don't spend the time finding the specific meaning, and attaching a strong enough reason why you must achieve the goal, you will most likely throw those hands up again and say, "I give up".

# 2
## FINDING STRONG ENOUGH
## REASONS WHY

*"Goals are the fuel in the furnace of achievement."* – Brian Tracy

I have a friend by the name of Jake. He and I go way back to our childhood days. Jake was always slightly overweight, and in grade school he got made fun of so he developed a complex over his weight and his eating habits. Eventually, Jake gained so much weight that he never wanted to eat in front of anyone else for fear that they would judge him. Anytime he and I went out to eat, I felt like he was watching me watch him to see if I was paying particular attention to just how much food he was consuming. I wasn't of course.

Then, a few years back, Jake went on this health kick. He cut out all the fat and bad carbs from his diet, upped his protein intake, and started hitting the gym. It was the four months before summer and Jake was able to shed just over 65 pounds. I was impressed, and so was Jake. I wanted to know how he pulled it off.

One night I met up with Jake and a few other friends to head out on the town, and I remember having a conversation with him about his weight loss. Before that night, I was always so skittish to talk about the weight subject around him, because anytime it would be brought up, I felt him cringe, and virtually shrivel up at the mere mention of it.

However, that night was different because I could tell that there was something different about Jake. He seemed like he was on an emotional high. He was vibrating positivity, and I had never seen him like that. It was impressive actually, seeing the once shy, overweight, childhood friend virtually transformed in front of my eyes.

I wanted to know what happened. What was so different that all of a sudden after 20 years of trying to lose weight, within a four-month period he had become like a man on a mission. This Jake didn't even seem like the same person. He walked different, he talked different, and it almost seemed like he had different mannerisms.

I wanted to know what was up so I simply got the nerve and asked him. I was expecting someone that would cower away again at the mere mention of weight, but this was different. It was a different response from an entirely different person. It was interesting to me, to say the least, to see this transformation, a transformation that I had recently only just experienced in myself.

I know that for me, the transformation didn't happen overnight. Going from someone who couldn't seem to hold onto anything steady, to becoming as solid as a rock, as earth shattering of a shift as that was, it occurred over time. Many different scenarios played out in the balance of my life that led me to that final ultimate shift on the inside. But it was the pain of hitting that emotional rock bottom that jarred me out of my ill set ways. I might have felt like I had woken up a new person but it didn't happen overnight.

So what happened to Jake?

What Jake explained to me was something that I think a lot of people experience. In life, we do much more to avoid pain than we do to gain pleasure. This is something called the pleasure principle, originally popularized by Freud, but touted by the likes of Anthony Robbins and many other success gurus. Jake was simply doing more to avoid pain than he was to gain pleasure.

Just before Jake's big health kick, he had paid a visit to the doctor. That day he had fainted at work and he was having chest pains, so naturally he went to the doctor to see what was going on. The news was the worst possible news he could have expected. Jake's weight was causing his heart to work overtime, and due to a genetic heart disease, his heart couldn't withstand the stress that the extra weight was putting it under. The doctor told Jake that he could potentially die within the year if he continued to put on weight, and didn't do something about it.

At first I was a little bit upset that Jake hadn't told me what was going on before, but then again he was always a pretty private person. But after the whole thing settled down in my mind, I guess I was a little bit impressed with what he had pulled off. Even though Jake was doing more to avoid pain than he was to gain pleasure, losing that much weight in such a short period of time is a feat in and of itself, so of course, I simply had to know every thought process he had to go through to get to that state of mind.

"It's easy," Jake, explained to me, "something just

happened all of a sudden inside me. It's like everything that I ever knew, or ever felt about food, changed in that one instant. I guess all of a sudden I had a reason I needed to lose weight rather than just wanting to lose weight. It really meant something to me this time."

I guess I looked at Jake with a complete look of bewilderment on my face, because I could read his response to my contorted facial reactions. This was almost identical to what I had felt about other areas of my life.

Jake continued, "But even though it felt like it happened overnight, everything led up to that point. The doctor's visit was just the straw that broke the camel's back. Every social cue that I had received before that, everything that I knew and felt deep down inside about food, and my emotional attachment to eating was there inside of me. I knew what to do I just could never succeed in doing it. I thought I had tried in the past, but when I saw what I did to lose the weight this time around, my efforts in the past paled in comparison. This time I was committed. I felt like a laser beam burrowing a hole through the old me. "

I was impressed to say the least because in life a lot of people set goals, but not a lot of people achieve them. Why is that? Well, just think about the pain versus pleasure paradigm for a minute. In the past haven't you done more to avoid pain than you have to gain pleasure?

In school, we cram before the night of a test. Why? We're doing more to avoid the pain of flunking a test than we are to gain the pleasure of procrastinating on the couch in front of a TV for just one more night. We do this in many areas of our lives, such as with taxes. We know that we have to get our taxes done, but most of us wait until the last minute. At that point, the balance of pain versus pleasure shifts from the pleasure of not having to deal with it, to the pain of having to suffer the consequences of not filing on time.

Everyone has been in these same, if not similar, situations, where the pain of not doing something begins to far outweigh the pleasure of doing something else in turn. It happens to everyone without fail. We've all partaken in it. But how do you go about avoiding becoming a victim of the pain versus pleasure paradigm? How do we set goals that we actually strive to achieve, rather than let wither away on some crumpled up piece of paper somewhere?

You have to attribute a strong enough reason why to do it, that's how. When people have a strong enough reason why they want to accomplish something, it propels them in a way like never before. For my friend, Jake, his strong enough reason why was the potential for death if he didn't take some course of action to restore health and wellness to his body by losing weight.

However, it doesn't take a potential for death in order not give up on goals in life. If you are able to find a strong enough reason why you must do something and that reason is powerful enough to reverse the pain pleasure paradigm, your goal achieving will become much more fluid, and automatic. You won't give up.

This is one of the primary requirements to successful goal setting, and if you're not in the habit of coming up with strong enough reasons why you want to achieve something, that may be why you've given up in the past.

If you truly have your heart's desire set on something, attach a strong enough reason why to it. Spend the time to figure out why you *need* to achieve something, as opposed to why you *want* to achieve something. If you make it a must, from a maybe, and attach a strong enough motivator to it, your chances for success will skyrocket. If you've never done this before, you'll be surprised as to just how much it will have you thinking deeply about your personal goals.

What do your goals really mean to you? Are they filled with the desire for monetary attainment? If they are, why do you want those things? Dig deep, question yourself until you can't question yourself anymore, and find the real reasons why you truly want to achieve something. Here are a few different motivators that you can attach to your goals to give them strong enough reasons why:

1.  **For family** – Many people will sacrifice just about anything for their family, and do just about anything. If family is important to you, attach a specific reason why your family is so important to the attainment of your goal. This will help you to not give up when the going gets tough. To me, family is vital, because without my family I would have nothing, and I think that most people can relate to that.

2.  **For freedom** – Freedom can be freedom from just about anything, but what most people think of when they hear freedom is monetary freedom. To be able to go anywhere, do anything, and be with anyone in the world that you choose can drive some people, but not all. For freedom to be a strong enough motivator you have to attach some very powerful reasons as to why you want that freedom so badly. If the pain of working harder exceeds the pleasure of having that freedom, you might find yourself giving up again.

3. **For faith** – Faith & religion can be extremely strong motivators for why people want to attain certain goals in their lives. If you are a strong believer in your own faith or religion, then dig deep down inside to see why your faith or religion would be so important to you as to be the primary motivator for your goals. Sometimes, faith and religion can be so strong as to help push you that last inch just when you're ready to give up.

4. **For survival** – People will do almost anything to survive; it's built into our genetic makeup. If you, like Jake, have a survival scenario, it could be one of the biggest factors that can motivate you to not give up on the goals that you set forth. Survival can mean a lot of things, and not just survival of yourself in terms of your life, but also for the survival of a cause, a group, a business, a passion, your financial survival, and just about any other thing. See if the survival of something, including yourself, is important enough to you, so as to push you to the attainment of your goals.

5. **For love** – Love is a very strong motivator. Wars have been waged over love, and people have given up their lives in the name of love. If you love something, or someone, and hold that thing or person near and dear to your heart, this could be one of the strongest motivators for the "why" of your goals. Whether it's love for your children, your spouse, or anything else, take a deep look at the love in your life, and see if crafting a reason in

the name of love can push you to achieve your dreams, and not give up.

No matter what your "why" is, it has to be a strong one. Any of these five categories can motivate, and inspire you to pursue your hopes and dreams without giving up, as long as you attribute it the right way to your goal. You just have to find the one that fits your particular goal, and situation, and you have to believe strongly enough in it to push you to the attainment of that goal.

For example, let's just say you wanted to have a net worth of at least a million dollars by the age of 40, 50 or whatever age it may be. Why do you want that million dollars (or euros, pounds; whatever other currency draws an equivalency to a lot of money in most people's eyes)? It's a question you have to ask yourself. Clearly it's not because you want more pieces of paper featuring historical dead presidents or royalty on them. What does that million dollars mean to you?

You might want a million dollars for family, to take care of and support your loved ones when they need you most. You could attribute a life of lack to not having the million dollars, and it represents being free from the stress of life and living in abundance. That million dollars could mean that your mother, father, wife, husband, or whoever, would never have to struggle, and work another day in their lives again. Whatever it is, you have to make some strong associations to why you want that goal, if you want to actually achieve it. You don't just want the million dollars to have it; you want it because it will bring you something.

You might also want a million dollars for freedom. The freedom that having a million dollars can bring you is boundless. You can go where you want, do what you want, and not be tied to living your life slaving away at a nine to five job that leaves you yearning for more of an insatiable life.

You may want a million dollars for faith, in order to be able to give to your church, or help those in need around you. You might also want the million dollars for survival, and security. As you can see here, the list can go on and on, but the more time you can actually spend attributing and associating a strong enough reason why to your hopes, and dreams, the more likely you will be to achieve them in the long run.

# 3

## ERADICATING LIMITING BEHAVIORS

*"Winning isn't everything, but wanting to win is."* – *Vince Lombardi*

Think back for a moment to a time in your life when you were on a role, and nothing could go wrong. You were unstoppable, completely on fire, and no matter what you did, everything turned out right. No, scratch that, more than just right, it turned out perfect, better than you could have even have ever expected.

Think back to that time in your life when you were juiced about everything, and rolling on an emotional high fueled by your inner most desires being actualized. Good things just seemed to happen all the time, every time, no matter what you did.

Can you remember that time? Good. Now make that picture bigger in your mind. Make it brighter and put it in full color. Imagine that picture now playing in front of you on a massive white screen in a grassy field set against a clear blue-sky backdrop. Then, imagine yourself sitting there in that grassy field, only a few feet from the giant screen looking up at it, watching the beautiful images of your life replay like a Hollywood movie.

Can you see yourself now? Look at the smile on your face. Look at how your eyes are twinkling. It's beautiful. Can you remember it? Can you remember this time and how life caught your breath as you inhaled in the passionate inspiration of the moment?

Can you see it there in front of you, sitting out in that field, in front of that giant screen, replaying life's beautiful moments in front of your eyes? It was a magical time, wasn't it? Nothing else seemed to matter to you then, did it? Nothing could have detracted you from the happiness you felt right then, and there.

It was as though all the bad in the world had greyed out, and fallen like dominos in the background, fading away into empty nothingness. None of that was important anymore. It was just you, and your happiness. That's all that you needed. That's all that you ever needed at that very moment in time.

Bring yourself back to that moment in time and close your eyes. Where were you? What were you doing? What were you laughing at? What was going through your mind at that precise instant? Can you remember the sensations that were running through your body? What did that feel like? Imagine that for a moment, and picture it. Really, picture it, and feel it as though you were reliving it.

If that time is as powerful a memory for you as it is for me, then that was a very chilling experience; an almost bitter sweet memory that's fondly held closer than you may have even realized. Maybe you forgot what that felt like to feel that way. I know I did for a while.

I remember that time in my own life, that happy time when I didn't feel so alone. But sometimes, I forget about that time, and other times like it, as I'm sure that we all do. Like any normal person, many of us simply get caught up living our lives, rushing from day to day just trying to cope, feeling utterly exhausted at the end of it.

For some reason, as human beings, the majority of us do this – we seem to ride this emotional rollercoaster of good times and bad. We all love to experience the good times. Those are the fun times when we're on a roll and life is going great, and we have friends around us, and everything seems to be perfect. But, we also all slip into the bad times; those dark times that you almost wished didn't exist. For some, the bad times are much worse than for others, and it's a dangerous place to be when you're all alone without a friend in sight.

The problem for most is that we allow the bad times to play on the screens of our lives, instead of the good times. Think back to that little exercise, and of seeing yourself on that screen, and how happy you were. Why is it that you're not at the happy place right now? What's changed since then?

What makes us, as human beings, slip back into these bad times when things are good? How do we allow things to get so bad before they can get so good? I know that I've had some very personal experiences with this in my life, just as nearly every one of us have, but it's all part of what I call our limiting behaviors. Why is it limiting?

Limiting behaviors can arise from many different situations. We tend to feel like we're stuck at times, and really have no other options, so we're dragged into this emotional bottom that feels like there's no end to it in sight. We allow the good times of our lives to slip away, feeling like we can't hold onto them. This happens to people all the time, and they begin to get discouraged, and down on their luck, and almost attract bad things in their lives.

So how do you avoid allowing these limiting behaviors to take over you? How do you get back to that happy place you replayed in your mind like a Hollywood movie? To do this you need to take the reigns on some of your behaviors, and patterns, that may cause you to dip down to the lows when you're riding those highs. It's okay, it happens to all of us, but unfortunately it can lead to a negative downward spiral.

In a book called *The Four Agreements: A Practical Guide to Personal Freedom*, author Don Miguel Ruiz suggests that to break through self-limiting behavior, we have to adhere to four agreements that we make with ourselves as to how we're going to live our lives. These four agreements will allow us to live life to its fullest, and always see that Hollywood movie playing in front of our eyes. But, instead of imagining it, we'll be experiencing it each and everyday.

Here are the four personal agreements that Ruiz suggests will help to offer a breakthrough from our limiting behaviors, and live a more fulfilled life:

1. **Be impeccable in your word** – By only speaking with honesty and integrity, in all situations in life, we can guide our lives in the direction of truth and love. This also involves avoiding any deprecating behaviors, such as gossiping, or spreading rumors about others. Only speak good things, and you will attract good things. Even when you are riding

life's highs, always do onto others what you would want them to do onto you.

2. **Don't take things personally** – It's important not to take things that other people do, personally. Everyone in life has their own agenda, but most of the times, we're found responding, and reacting to the actions of both friends, and foes, and it entrenches our entire lives. People have their own skewed realities about life and other people around them so it's important that you not put yourself through needless suffering by focusing on their actions.

3. **Don't make any assumptions** – You know what they say about assumptions don't you? They make an ass out of you and me. Making assumptions is never a good idea, because you never really know what a person's intentions are. The more you take to creating your own assumptions in your own mind, the more you risk partaking in sadness, and drama. Don't assume anything. This one agreement can completely transform your life.

4. **Always do your best** – You have to always strive to do your best, no matter what. You have to turn off all the noise out there in the world, and focus on you, and everything that you can do to improve your own life. Don't live your life in constant reaction to what other people say or do. Be yourself, and believe in yourself. Even when the odds seem like they're stacked up against you,

do your best anyways, and good things will eventually come your way.

I know that it's hard to try and live by these four agreements all the time, but you have to make a conscious, and concerted effort to try and shift your patterns, in order to eliminate limiting behaviors. Just imagine how much better our lives would be if we could all keep our word, not take things personally, not make assumptions, and always do our best. The world would be a much better place.

Focus on yourself, and not the others around you. By only worrying about your side of the street, you will make significant strides into eradicating all the deprecating thoughts and behaviors in your life. You will be on the road to not giving up.

# 4

## GOAL SETTING WORKSHOP

*"Our goals can only be reached through a vehicle of a plan, in which we must fervently believe, and upon which we must vigorously act. There is no other route to success." – Stephen A. Brennan*

"Mike, should I grab this one?" I was pointing to the last box left in the large empty dining room. It was moving day for Mike, and I was offering a helping hand as friends usually do.

"No, let me get that one. You've done enough," he said.

I had never seen Mike like this before in my entire life. It was as if you had packed 10 years onto a man within one year, then weighed him down with all the grief and sorrow of rejection and failure. His walk was now a head held low, shoulders hunched, and eyes to the ground. It was sad to see. "I really don't mind, Mike. Whatever you need, I'm here to help."

"What I need is a million dollars. Have an extra million dollars lying around you could loan me?" Mike slightly chuckled to himself, but I knew he was being half serious.

Mike had hit some hard times in his life. Things weren't going good at all. From the heydays when he was soaring on top of the world and could do no wrong, to this, an almost completely opposite person who couldn't hold his head up when he spoke to you. It was a dramatic shift.

What happened to, Mike?

Mike was my best friend from high school. He and I would share everything, go everywhere, and do everything together, and for the longest time we were inseparable. Some years passed, I got married and divorced, and Mike seemed to be out there still enjoying his life, and living it up. I was constantly seeing photos of him with pretty girls, soaking up the nightlife in whatever city he happened to be in at the time.

Mike was a highflying financial trader, and for a while he was considered the golden boy at his firm. He could do no wrong. Then one-day disaster hit, and the markets tanked. Everyone lost out, but Mike was highly leveraged on margin. He had borrowed money to make poor risky investments for himself, and his clients, that completely fizzled when the market dropped through the floor.

Mike had departed from even his own words on how to win in investing by making stable investments for the long term. Mike got cocky and stopped paying attention to the details, and because of it he lost his shirt.

Instead of trying to prop himself back up, Mike launched into a tirade of addictive behavior. I had never seen him like that, and it was frightening in fact. One day, he explained to me just all the things he had been doing from the booze, to the drugs, and everything else. It was as though he pushed himself deeper, and deeper into the rabbit hole.

To make matters worse, Mike began borrowing money from loan sharks. In fact, I didn't even think loan sharks still existed, but somehow, Mike found them, and borrowed everything he could from them. They probably remembered him from his highflying days of making unlimited amounts of cash for himself, and his clients, but things were different now.

This all led to one disastrous rock bottom like I had never seen anyone hit before. It was painful to watch, because the Mike from just a few short years ago was the guy that always had lots of goals that he was driven to accomplish. Mike was able to achieve most of his goals but it was at the expense of a lot of other meaningful things in his life. He trampled on everything, and everyone along the way to reach the top, and, when he hit bottom, there was almost no one there to help him back up.

I had a conversation with Mike a couple of years after he had gotten clean and sober, and rebuilt his trading portfolio back up again, to find out more about the mystery of what had happened to his life, and how he had gone through these dramatic shifts. He explained to me, that while he always had these grand goals in his life, they never really meant something deeply rooted to him. His goals of money and power all stemmed from his desire to show everyone up that doubted him. This, I believe was one of the things that did him in.

I think that when you set goals in life, they have to be meaningful, and they have to have important reasons behind them. Sure, we can go out there and achieve, achieve, achieve, but without there being something beyond just the superficial achievements, success will be very fleeting. It will be easy to let go and give up on something that didn't actually mean that much in the first place. My friend, Mike, never attributed a deep meaning to his goals.

We spoke for a while about goal setting, and it was an interesting conversation, to say the least. I told him about my goals, and he expressed his newly found, renewed sense of goals. However, these new goals that he had adopted, while still large, were rooted in very different things. He had developed extremely strong meanings, and reasons as to why he wanted to achieve those goals.

I was impressed. Mike was a new man and it seemed as though he had crafted a solid personal foundation for real lasting success in his life. He had figured out a way not to give up. During that conversation we both went over what it took to set goals, and how to set goals that you won't give up on. Here's the list of 6 steps that we came up with:

1.  Be very specific when setting your goals.

2.  Write your goals down somewhere, anywhere.

3.  Give yourself ample time to reach your goals.

4.  Cast out any doubts for not achieving your goals.

5.  Keep your goals to yourself.

6.  Eliminate stress from the recipe.

# BE VERY SPECIFIC WHEN SETTING YOUR GOALS

When you begin your goal setting you need to be very specific about your goals. You have to not only know exactly what you want to achieve, you have to say exactly when you want it. Don't just say you want a million dollars, say exactly when you want that million dollars by. Take the time to specifically brainstorm what you will do to earn the million dollars.

What I've found also works best for goals, are to break them apart. Take the long-term goal, and set a date, then work backwards, creating shorter-term goals for the interim periods. For example, if I wanted to make a million dollars in the next two years, I would need to figure out what I was going to do to make that million dollars, and break it apart into smaller intervals.

Earning a million dollars in two years means, making $250,000 every six months, or $41,667 per month. Yes, this is a lot of money, but when you break that million dollars down into smaller amounts, then tackle those smaller amounts, the notion is a lot more manageable. You can do this as a daily, weekly, or monthly goal, just based on how specific you want to get.

Let's say for example, you want to lost weight like my friend Jake, and you have a target of 40 pounds (just over 18 kilograms) within 6 months. Well, within that 6-month period, you'll know that you'll need to drop approximately 7 pounds per month to hit that target. If you take that 7 pounds and divide it into weeks, then the weekly weight loss comes to 1.75 pounds per week, which sounds a lot more manageable than when you think of 40 pounds all at once.

Furthermore, when you learn facts like understanding that 3500 calories is approximately equivalent to one pound of body fat (or 7700 calories in one kilo), and you figure out just how many calories your body burns per day versus what you eat, you can create a detailed road map to the specific amount of calorie intake you need to have, or burn, in order to reach your goal. Does this make sense? Hopefully it does.

# WRITE YOUR GOALS DOWN SOMEWHERE, ANYWHERE

Something dramatic happens when you physically take to the task of writing down your goals. A mental shift occurs inside of you, and the goal becomes all that much more real. The simple solidification that occurs in your mind is very definite, making the goal that much more tangible.

Whether you take to writing your goals down on a piece of paper in a notepad, on your laptop computer, or even on your mobile phone, it's an important step to take in order to not give up on your goals. The physical act of writing your goals also helps you to be specific, and set specific dates, on paper, just when you must achieve parts of your long-term, and short-term goals.

If you've set goals in the past, with just the idea or notion of the goal in your mind, it's not enough. You need to solidify the goals on paper, or digital format, with the specific outline of what the goal is, how you will achieve it, and what dates you will achieve them on. This will make a huge difference in your ability to not give up on your goals.

Place the goals somewhere that you can read them, and reference them each day before you go to bed, and after you wake up. This will allow you to have a moving target for the day, week, month, and year on what specific tasks need to be accomplished for your goals, and allows you to make adjustments as you go along.

# GIVE YOURSELF AMPLE TIME TO REACH YOUR GOALS

It's important to give yourself ample time to reach your goals, whatever they may be. If you've never worked out a day in your life, don't say that you're going to work out 5 days a week, and run a marathon in a month. Try to build up to a goal like that. Start with twice a week, for example, for the first 8 weeks then move up to three, or four times a week, from there. Then, maybe commit yourself to running a half marathon within 6 months, then a full marathon within 1 year.

Doing this not only helps you build confidence it helps to build momentum. When you begin to see results, you will naturally want to keep increasing your input to see more output. As time goes by, assess your goals, and see which ones you're making progress on, and which ones you're not.

Take the time to adjust your short-term goals if

necessary in order to reach your long-term goals. If you need to, adjust your long-term goals as well. Don't feel like you can't change your goals as soon as you've finished writing them for the first time. Allow them to be fluid, and dynamic.

If you want to earn a million dollars in two years, what will you do to earn an extra $10,000 per month in the next three months, for example? How will you go from earning a little, to a lot? What steps will you take? Break it down, but give yourself time for the large goals, and instead break them apart into shorter goals, spaced out in the longer term. This will lead to your eventual success no matter what you set out to do and achieve.

Once you start setting your goals, and begin the path to achieving them, you'll have a better sense of what amount of effort your goals will take. Achieving your goals is going to require consistent daily action, so allow yourself time to get there. Don't be too hard on yourself, even if you falter the first few times. Stay committed, and don't give up, and over time you will begin to see incredible results.

# CAST OUT ANY DOUBTS FOR NOT ACHIEVING YOUR GOALS

This step combines taking the meanings that you developed for your goals, and combining them with the strong enough reasons why you must accomplish them. Cast out any other doubts that you might have about your ability to accomplish your goals.

Anytime you allow lingering beliefs that limit you to reside in your mind, they put up small barriers in your road to success. Don't allow life to throw up these barriers for you. Cast out any doubts that you may have about your ability, and capability, to accomplish something.

Human beings have made incredible advances in the past century. Just imagine the things that can be done now that were once just science fiction, or considered magic. You can do anything that you put your mind to, literally, anything. And although reaching your goals may be hard, the journey is what defines us. Spend the time wisely, and don't sweat the small stuff. A little bit of progress each day, leads to a lot of progress in the end.

# KEEP YOUR GOALS TO YOURSELF

In 2009, a man by the name of Peter Gollwitzer, did a study on 163 people in 4 separate tests. He split the group in half, and asked one half to announce their goals, and the other half, not to announce their goals. And then spend the next 45 minutes, or however long it took, working on those goals in a room, and stop when they felt like they were done.

The outcome of this test, was that the half that didn't announce their goals, spent the full 45 minutes working on their goals. At the end of the test, they said they had a lot to work on in order to achieve the goals that they had in their lives.

The other half, the ones that did announce their goals, spent on average 33 minutes outlining their goals before finishing. At the end of the test, they too were asked how they felt about their goals, and said that they felt much closer to achieving them.

What happens when you announce your goals is that your mind mistakes talking, for doing. When you announce it, you receive acknowledgment of your goal almost as if it was already completed. This acknowledgement tricks your mind into thinking that the goal has already been attained, forcing you to work much less harder on those goals.

Of course, it's been said in rare cases that announcing something, or saying something in the literal, brings it into reality, bringing you one step closer to having those goals. However, this, for the most part does not work. Do not announce your goals to the world, otherwise, risk the potential for giving up.

If you need to vocalize your goals, do it in a way where you aren't announcing the goal, to the whole world through social media. For example, if you're trying to lose weight, and your goal is to run a marathon, instead of saying that, tell one person that you need to run a marathon, so you have to train 5 times a week, and if you don't, that they should kick your butt. This will give you some accountability in your goal as well. Make sense?

# ELIMINATE STRESS FROM THE RECIPE

Stress is the silent killer. The more stress you have in your life, the more likely you are going to be to crack under pressure. In the pursuit of your goals, it's important to try and cut out all of the stress that you possibly can. This doesn't mean that you have to isolate yourself from the world. It just means that you need to spend the time designing your day for an optimized reduction in stress levels.

In order to eliminate stress from your life, you have to first identify the stressors in your life. Spend 10 minutes writing down what stresses you out, and make a top-10 list out of these. Then, go through this list and weed out what things can be removed. Do you have some unnecessary activities or commitments that you can easily untangle yourself from? Are there some activities that you do that may be causing you a great deal of stress? Once you see the list in front you, it will be much easier to identify your stressors.

No matter what you do, some days are going to be harder than others. Stress is a part of our lives, however, stress at intolerable levels, should not be part of the recipe. If you are in a high stress situation, whether at home or at work, consider weighing your options for eliminating some of that stress. If you sit down and analyze it, you'll be able to come up with solutions to just about any stressors.

Here are some examples of stressors in your life you can try to identify, and remove, to live a less chaotic life that will see your pursuit of goals end in achievement, and not giving up:

1. **Disorganization** – This can stress just about anyone out, but it is a simple area of your life to tackle with just a few minutes each day. If your home, or office is disorganized, begin by organizing the areas you spend the most time in. Do a little bit of organization each time. You will be surprised at how much better you will feel living or working in a visually clutter-free environment.

2. **Unnecessary commitments** – This can be an enormous burden on some people who don't really know how to say no. If you have some unnecessary commitments in your life, see if you can work on easing some of this so that you don't feel the weight of these pressing down on your shoulders. Relinquishing yourself from these will help you to create a more Zen-like peace of mind, and live a more stress free life.

3. **Multi-tasking** – Although many of us pride ourselves on our ability to multi-task, this can be detrimental to our mental well-being, and be a major cause of stress in our lives. If you're trying to tackle too many things at once, see if you can reduce some of that workload on yourself.

4. **Scheduling** – Your schedule may be causing you unneeded stress. It's not necessary to have to schedule every minute of your life. If you're a chronic scheduler, try to get into the habit of allowing yourself more periods of unscheduled time where you get to work on the tasks that are important to your future success, and not just things that need your immediate attention.

5. **Difficult people** – Difficult people can be one of the biggest causes of stress in our lives. Learning to avoid difficult people is one of the best ways that you can go about eliminating stress from your life. Instead of confronting difficult people, and constantly worrying about what they have to say, or what they do, if at all possible, just try to avoid them altogether. Don't allow yourself to get caught up in the limiting behavior of constantly worrying about other people's actions. Just focus on you.

6. **Pace of life** – How fast-paced is your life? How much are you always on the go? If life is very fast-paced for you, consider slowing it down a bit.

Take the time to enjoy the simpler things. Slowly chew and savior your food when you eat it, or step out and take a leisurely stroll beneath the sun in a park. Life isn't all about doing and achieving, it's also about the journey, and enjoying the moment.

7.  **Exercise** – Not only can exercise help eliminate some stress, it also helps to prevent it as well. Not only is exercise good for your physical well-being, but it also gives you time to yourself to think about your goals, and mentally prioritize the day's events. Pick a time each day, or certain days each week, where you commit to at least 30 minutes of light activity. That small amount of motion will create momentum, and build upon itself. You'll be surprised at just how much stress is eliminated in your life with a little bit of exercise.

8.  **Health habits** – Your diet is an enormous factor on the levels of stress that your body will tend to experience at any given moment. You've heard the saying that you are what you eat, but more importantly, the amount of time and energy that your body requires to process the food that you put into it, is enormous. When your body is busy processing refined sugars, carbohydrates, and high fatty foods, it makes you feel sluggish, and not alert enough to help tackle the day's tasks. Of course, this also extends into things like alcohol consumption, cigarette smoking, and all other detrimental health-related activities.

9. **To-do lists** – Are you a chronic to-do list creator? Aside from setting goals and having a main goal sheet, how many to-do lists do you actually create in your life? If your to-do list is long, eliminate things that you feel you can comfortably eliminate, or that may seem extraneous. If you have a lot of small to-dos on your list, try to batch them together into one, and simplify your list. You'll be surprised at just how much stress you alleviate by having smaller to-do lists in your life.

10. **Community** - If you're not into your community, or giving back to help others, this is something you should do immediately. Giving always makes you feel grateful for what you have, and getting in the habit of giving, is one of the best practices for helping you put things in perspective, and eliminate stress in your life. Be grateful, and give back to others in your community, and you'll be surprised at just how much of an emotional, and mental boost, you get from doing this.

# 5

## THE FIVE STEPS TO MASSIVE ACTION

*"Obstacles are those things you see when you take your eyes off your goals." – Sydney Smith*

"How did you do it, Mike? How did you dig yourself out of that hole?"

"It was tough. No, actually, it wasn't just tough, it was seemingly impossible at the time, but somehow I managed to climb out. It took me a while, but I pulled it off."

"Yes, but how? What did you do?" Mike was penniless. Not only was he penniless, but he had also been left in debt to the tune of five hundred thousand dollars. Now, if that isn't heavy, I'm not sure what is.

"I just took it one day at a time. That's all I could do. One day at a time. There were days when I thought I wanted to end it all, but then I thought about my son, and that saw me through. I couldn't imagine him growing up without a father, so I persevered, and I pushed through it. I spent months struggling through sleepless nights, and agonizing days. I can't tell you how hard it was, and I'm not quite sure how I made it through, but I did."

Not only was it impressive, it was a near miracle. Mike never explained to me exactly what he did to pull himself free from just over a one-half-million dollars in debt, to now being the number one most successful trader at his firm. But Mike did tell me one thing; he took it "One day at a time."

Sometimes in life, you have to tackle things one day at a time. That massive action needs to just focus on the task at hand. By doing that, and not allowing yourself to get overwhelmed, day by day you persevere, and make just a little bit more progress. Eventually, you break through the barriers that were holding you back, and make incredible strides and accomplish things that you yourself never even could have dreamed would be possible before.

Think about a man or a woman who begins a task and decides that he wants to increase his knowledge of that task by 1% each day. Think about what that would do for you, if you were able to increase by 1% each day. What would happen is that each day you would get more and more educated, and insightful about that field, until one day you exploded into mastery level. The key is that you have to take massive action, and you have to believe in yourself.

You know, human beings can accomplish anything. Whatever we set our minds to, we can do. Just think about that for a moment, and think about how far we have come as a race, and just how much progress has been made. Did you know that in the last 100 years, more technological advances have been made than in all of time? Can you possibly imagine what the next 100 years will hold? The ideas are limitless.

Everything that we have today, everything that we are, all started with a simple thought. That simple thought evolved until it grew, and became something tangible. It started with the burning desire to learn something, make something, or do something. Revolutions were fought, freedom was won, governments toppled, all in the name of progress and education, and it all happened by taking massive action.

If you think that you can't accomplish your hopes and dreams by taking massive action, think again. The examples are all around you, and all you have to do is look. J.K. Rowling had the idea for the first Harry Potter book in 1990. It took her 7 years to publish that first novel, and in that period of time she suffered the loss of her mother, and was living on social security from the government. Today, she is the most successful author in the UK, with upwards of 500 million copies of the Harry Potter books sold worldwide.

In life, none of your goals are going to happen on their own. What's more is that, none of your goals are going to happen without taking massive action. In the past, if you've given up on something and couldn't accomplish it, then you didn't take massive action, because taking massive action is the absolute foundational core to not giving up.

You know the saying about Rome of course, it wasn't built in a day, and your goals, although may seem very far away right now, will inch closer and closer to you each and every day that you apply a little bit of action towards the attainment of them.

However, some people simply just don't know where to start when it comes to taking massive action towards the attainment of their goals. They feel overwhelmed. With so much on people's plates, they just don't just how to kick things into high gear. If you're one of these people, and you feel stuck in your life with the inability to take action, here are a few key pointers that will help you to get things going.

Tips for taking massive action:

1. **Identify the goal** – The first thing that you need to do is identify the goal that you're going to start taking massive action on. This must be from one of the goals set in the goal-setting workshop discussed in the previous chapter.

2. **15-minute brainstorm session** – Take your goal and take a look at all the short-term goals that you set for yourself within that goal. If you set weekly goals, or even daily goals, start with that. What you want to do is spend 15 minutes brainstorming everything you can possibly do right now to achieve that goal. No matter how small it is you must be able to do it right now.

3. **Identify with the 80/20 rule** – The 80/20 rule stems from something called the Pareto Principle (or the law of the vital few), which states that 80% of the effects, come from 20% of the causes. You need to identify what those 20% of the causes, or

actions are, and tackle those immediately. For example, if one of your goals is to own your own business, start by logging onto your local business portal on the Internet to begin conducting a business name search to see what names are available. Starting with picking a name can lead to registering a business, and beyond.

4. **Use the 5-minute timer method** – This is an excellent method for breaking the pattern of inability to act. Take a timer (you can use your cell phone or a stop watch), and set it to 5 minutes. Take the task that you've identified that you need to do, and begin doing it and time yourself for 5 minutes. For example, if one of your goals is to get organized, start by cleaning your room. Turn the timer on, and go. Don't think about it, just do it. You'll realize that you will end up spending much more time than 5 minutes on it, in most cases. Action will lead to more action, and you need to act now.

5. **Rinse & repeat** – By repeating the first four steps over and over again with the simple application of breaking things down into smaller parts, you will be able to successfully tackle just about any task. What's more, is that as soon as you begin building some momentum, you will notice yourself taking even more action, and producing even more results. Success begets success, but it all starts with action. Simple steps today, will lead to large results tomorrow.

# 6
# FOUR MAGICAL INGREDIENTS TO ACHIEVING YOUR GOALS

*"Nothing can stop the man with the right mental attitude from achieving his goal; nothing on earth can help the man with the wrong mental attitude."* – Thomas Jefferson

I looked up at my success wall, as I liked to call it, and I felt proud. In front of me hung photos of the places I wanted to go, the people I wanted to meet, and the things I wanted to do. There were pictures of beautiful sunsets, fast cars, exotic faraway lands, and families laughing on the beach. It was what I wanted in life. It was my success wall.

I was 22 at the time, living and working from home running a graphic and design freelance firm. I was juiced about life and I remember it vividly. That wall meant so much to me. I would painstakingly cut out photos, and carefully affix them to just the right places on the wall so that my eye traveled in a direction that told a story.

Do you know the kind of wall I'm talking about?

If you don't know what a success wall is, it's a wall filled with the positive emotional connectors to the goals of your life. Once you've set your goals, and you've begun working on your limiting behaviors, you need a constant daily visual reminder of your goals, beyond just the review of your goal list on a daily basis.

There's something about looking up at a wall filled with images that represent your hopes and your dreams; there's something very powerful about it. My wall was located in my home office, in a spare bedroom at the time, and it was a large corkboard that bore all the photos, and words, that represented my goals. Aside from cutting out photos from magazines, I printed off large text letters from my computer that featured, and epitomized the goal. I had different sections dedicated to the different goals of my life, and everything was one big happy image right in front of my eyes.

When you look up at a wall like that, something happens to you internally that you don't realize is happening. It constantly reminds you of what you're doing and why you're doing it, and it's the perfect opportunity to display your hopes and dreams visually for your mind's eye to read on a constant basis. There's something about the photos that transcends the mere words that represents your goal. They're powerful and impactful.

In life, sometimes we need all the help we can get in order to constantly seek and realize our goals, and not give up. A success wall is the visual representation of your dreams that stem from the positive emotional connectors that you affix to them. In life, all of us need a little bit of hope and inspiration on a daily basis. Whatever drives you to succeed, and make you become the person you want to, should be represented visually as a constant reminder.

Not giving up takes hard work, but there are some ingredients to goal setting, and achieving, that if applied, can help you realize your hopes and dreams much sooner. Here's a list of what I call the four magical ingredients you'll need to achieve your own personal goals and not giving up.

1. **Positive emotional connectors** – To come up with your positive emotional connectors, go through your list of goals, and take a look and see what direct emotional result will come from the achievement of your goal. If you have a goal that will make you happy, list that off, or one that will make you feel at peace, then list that off. Take one or two words that symbolize this emotional connector, and print them off in big fonts for your own success wall. Finding these emotional connectors is important to the next step of finding visual representations.

2. **Visual representations** – This isn't just cutting out photos of fast cars, and big houses, it goes beyond that. From the first step of identifying the positive emotional connectors to the achievement of your goals, find photos that symbolize those emotional connectors. If you don't have magazines lying around, use a Website like Pintrest.com to search for photos, and print them off on your printer. It's very important to have these on your success wall in a place that you can see everyday. If you have a home office and work from home, put your success wall where you can look at it every time you bring your head up from the computer screen. If you work at an office,

place it there if you can, or find some other place in your home. Wherever you place it, simply just decide to do it, and do it now.

3. **Real accountability** – Pick one person very close to you, and tell them about your goal. Do not announce it to anyone else. Make that one person hold you responsible for following through with your goal. This will help you to not give up by creating accountability to someone that is close to you. You can tell your spouse, your significant other, or a close friend. Just find one person to tell, and make sure that they hold you accountable.

4. **Sincere patience** – Achieving your goals takes patience, and this is the final ingredient to the recipe of success. You cannot force something to happen before it's intended time, however, if you take consistent action towards the attainment of that goal, then over time, you will succeed. Giving up or throwing the towel in before this happens is not an option. Never give up. Never surrender. Just have a bit of patience.

# 7

## MIRRORING SUCCESS

*"Life is a mirror and will reflect back to the thinker what he thinks into It." – Ernest Holmes*

It's easy to talk about wanting to succeed at something and not give up, but it's much harder to do it. People get bored of working on the same arduous task day in and day out. They just want to have a good time, see their friends, eat whatever food they like, and not worry about the day-to-day stresses of trying to constantly achieve. Of course, these same people also secretly want success in their lives, but don't want to have to work for it.

This is typical of our society. We want it all but we don't want to work for it. I know, I've been there. I know how it feels. There was a time in my life where I let life control me and I didn't take control of my life. I slipped into that time after a period of constantly striving to achieve, but I got burnt out.

We all get burnt out sometimes in life. It's hard to keep pushing and pushing against what seems like it's a brick wall that won't budge. What's worse is that setbacks in life can completely devastate a person's will to succeed, forcing him or her to throw in the towel and give up. But, the best way to really find success is, to mirror it.

When you mirror success, you look to those who came before you; you look to those that fought the long hard road to achieve seemingly insurmountable goals in the face of so many obstacles. There are so many stories in our history about famous people who have achieved their goals, that the Internet is literally littered with them.

Everyone likes to hear the story about someone overcoming obstacles to achieve their dreams. Jim Carrey, who is now well known around the world, dropped out of high school at the young age of 16 years old. In Canada, Carrey and his family lived in a camper van, and he worked for 8 hours a day at a tire factory just to try to help make ends meet.

Jim Carrey moved to LA, and began shadowing Rodney Dangerfield, a famous comedian, in hopes that he would hit it big himself. Carrey is notoriously known for writing himself a check for 10 million dollars before he became famous. He dated the check for Thanksgiving, 1995, and he carried this check around with him everywhere he went. Eventually, the check began to deteriorate in his pocket, but then, just before Thanksgiving, 1995, he found out he would be getting the role for Dumb & Dumber that would earn him 10 million dollars.

Jim Carrey placed that check for 10 million dollars into the casket for his father when he was buried, because it was a dream that they had together. This goes to show you what you can accomplish when you don't give up. For years, as a struggling comedian, Jim didn't know how he was going to succeed, he just knew that he was going to succeed. It wasn't a *should* for him, it was a *must*.

Jim Carrey's simple act of writing that check was a very powerful silent commitment to himself. Writing that check created an internal shift that set a whole string of actions into motion towards the attainment of his goal. It was a powerful practice in the art of the Law of Attraction, but the simple act of writing it down made it more real and tangible for him. He carried that check with him everywhere he went as a constant reminder of the commitment he made to himself, and his father, that he would succeed in the competitive entertainment industry.

Before Mark Wahlberg became the well known actor and director that he is today, he too dropped out of high school, but at the age of 14. However, instead of initially pursuing his dreams, he resorted to stealing and dealing drugs, eventually landing himself in jail for 50 days. It's during those 50 days that Wahlberg says, that the emotional shift happened for him. His brother who had gotten a record deal at the time, helped to pull him into the music business, and he became "Marky Mark" a successful rapper who then parlayed that success into an acting career.

There are stories of success all around us, and simply opening ones eyes can show you the trials and tribulations that people had to endure in order to get to where they are today. The problem is that most people only get to see the end result of all that hard work. They don't see all the work that went before it.

When you see someone famous, you simply think how lucky they are, and how he or she got such a big break in life. What you don't see are the years of blood, sweat, and tears, and of not getting a paycheck for doing something they loved until they final made the enormous breakthroughs that brought them to where they are today.

In looking at successful people that are well known, it's simple to spot some characteristics that stand out, which helped them to persevere and not give up. Like Jim Carrey and Mark Wahlberg, countless other celebrities have similar stories of pushing through, even when the times were so tough, to finally getting a big break. However, aside from just the celebrities, there are millions upon millions of average people who accomplish their goals, as well, in a similar way.

Ask almost anyone you know that's succeeded and they'll tell you that just before they were about to give up, just when they thought they couldn't push anymore, finally it happened – they broke through.

Mirroring the success of others can work to help you to realize your own potential. While you may have heard it before, your possibilities of what you can do with your life truly are limitless. There are absolutely no barriers holding you back from living the life of your dreams other than the ones you create for yourself.

# 8

## HOW NOT TO GIVE UP

*"I do not think that there is any other quality so essential to success of any kind as the quality of perseverance. It overcomes almost everything, even nature." – John D. Rockefeller*

If at first you don't succeed try, and try again.

We've all heard this before in our lives, probably countless more times than we can even remember. However, how true is this statement? You have to realize that many people in life have failed, in fact, ask a professional athlete who's successful in their sport, about some great statistic related to their game play, and they will quickly point out how many more times they failed at doing the same thing.

Considered to be one of the best basketball players to have ever graced the courts, Michael Jordan is one such professional athlete who feels this way. In a quote he says, "I've missed more than 9000 shots in my career. I've lost almost 300 games. 26 times, I've been trusted to take the game winning shot, and missed. I've failed over, and over, and over, again in my life. And that is why I succeed."

In life, without trying, you won't fail. But success can only really come to those who fail. Think about everything, and everyone in life, who has achieved some great measure of success. Many of them have failed, and fallen flat on their faces more times than even they would like to admit. It's okay to fail. I've failed many times, just as has the next person. However, it's not about failing that's important, it's about what you do after you fail that's important.

When Thomas Edison was inventing the light bulb, he had failed over 9,000 times when a young reporter famously interviewed him before succeeding with his invention. That young reporter asked Mr. Edison what it felt like to have failed so many times already in trying to invent the light bulb, and asked him why he hadn't given up yet. Mr. Edison replied, "Young man, why would I feel like a failure? And why would I ever give up? I now know definitively over 9,000 ways that an electric light bulb will not work. Success is almost in my grasp."

Edison finally succeeding in inventing the light bulb, but it took him over 10,000 attempts to get it right. Could you possibly imagine failing at something over 10,000 times before succeeding? How many people do you think that would detract from achieving a certain goal? Most people would quit after only a handful of attempts. This trait of tenacity, and perseverance, is seen clear across the board when it comes to successful people who have failed many times before they succeeded.

To some people, the simple fear of failure scares them. Yes, you can be afraid to fail, but not to the extent that it stifles your actions. You must fail to succeed, and in fact you must fail many times over. Failure is a sign that success is nearing. However, for some, finding the tenacity to get up and try again when they fail multiple times over, is seen as the biggest difficulty.

When you look at what others have endured and struggled through to get where they are, you come to the realization that nothing in life will come easy without some failure. There was always some hard work done, somewhere by someone in order to reach success. They had to fail first before they succeeded, but they never gave up.

In life, you can't give up. You have to push through and keep going. By setting goals, eradicating your limiting behaviors, taking massive action, and modifying your approach as you go along, you too can achieve success, and not find yourself giving up. But along the road, you will encounter some failures, and that's natural.

Don't be afraid to press on, and don't be afraid to keep pursuing something even if it feels like it is completely out of reach for you today. Keep pushing, pushing, and pushing through your limitations until you succeed. Don't ever give up because when you do finally reach that goal, it will be one of the sweetest victories you have ever tasted.

Always hold onto your hopes and your dreams, and don't ever allow anyone to take them away from you. You can do anything your heart desires. You can achieve anything you put your mind to. I know you can. *You know you can.*

# THANK YOU

If you enjoyed the book, I would really appreciate it if you could take a few moments and share your thoughts by posting a review on Amazon. If this book inspired you in any way shape or form, I would love to hear about it in a book review.

I hope that my care and sincerity come across in my writing because in the end I write to bring value to other people's lives. I hope that this book has brought some value to your life. I truly do.

Here is the link that you can use to post a review on Amazon for this book - http://www.amazon.com/dp/B00BSB02KI

I wish you all the best in the pursuit of your hopes and dreams. Never allow anyone make you give up. Never.

-RL Adams

## OTHER BOOKS IN THIS SERIES

This book is the first of six books in the *Inspirational Books Series* of personal development books that I've released. You can check out all the books in the series that are available, in the proceeding list:

- How Not to Give Up – A Motivational & Inspirational Guide to Goal Setting & Achieving your Dreams (Volume 1)

- The Silk Merchant – Ancient Words of Wisdom to Help you Live a Better Life Today (Volume 2)

- Have a Little Hope – An Inspirational Guide to Discovering What Hope is and How to Have More of it in Your Life (Volume 3)

- <u>Breakthrough</u> – Live an Inspired Life, Overcome your Obstacles and Accomplish your Dreams (Volume 4)

- <u>How to be Happy</u> – An Inspirational Guide to Discovering What Happiness is and How to Have More of it in your Life (Volume 5)

- <u>Move Mountains</u> – How to Achieve Anything in your Life with the Power of Positive Thinking (Volume 6)

28603513R00043

Made in the USA
Lexington, KY
22 December 2013